Lessons
from Jesus

LUKE

New Community Bible Study Series

Old Testament
Exodus: Journey toward God
1 and 2 Samuel: Growing a Heart for God
Nehemiah: Overcoming Challenges
Psalms Vol. 1: Encountering God
Psalms Vol. 2: Life-Changing Lessons
Daniel: Pursuing Integrity

New Testament
Sermon on the Mount 1: Connect with God
Sermon on the Mount 2: Connect with Others
The Lord's Prayer: Praying with Power
Parables: Imagine Life God's Way
Luke: Lessons from Jesus
Acts: Build Community
Romans: Find Freedom
2 Corinthians: Serving from the Heart
Philippians: Run the Race
Colossians: Discover the New You
James: Live Wisely
1 Peter: Stand Strong
1 John: Love Each Other
Revelation: Experience God's Power

BILL HYBELS

WITH KEVIN & SHERRY HARNEY

New Community
KNOWING. LOVING. SERVING. CELEBRATING.

Lessons
from Jesus

LUKE

ZONDERVAN®

WILLOW
Willow Creek Resources

ZONDERVAN.com/
AUTHORTRACKER
follow your favorite authors

Luke: Lessons from Jesus
Copyright © 2008 by Willow Creek Association

Requests for information should be addressed to:

Zondervan, *Grand Rapids, Michigan* 49530

ISBN 978-0-310-28056-9

Interior design by Sherri Hoffman

Printed in the United States of America

08 09 10 11 12 13 14 • 21 20 19 18 17 16 15 14 13 12 11 10 9 8 7 6 5 4 3 2 1

CONTENTS

New Community
BIBLE STUDY SERIES

God has created us for community. This need is built into the very fiber of our being, the DNA of our spirit. As Christians, our deepest desire is to see the truth of God's Word as it influences our relationships with others. We long for a dynamic encounter with God's Word, intimate closeness with his people, and radical transformation of our lives. But how can we accomplish those three difficult tasks?

The New Community Bible Study Series creates a place for all of this to happen. In-depth Bible study, community-building opportunities, and life-changing applications are all built into every session of this small group study guide.

How to Build Community

How do we build a strong, healthy Christian community? The whole concept for this study grows out of a fundamental understanding of Christian community that is dynamic and transformational. We believe that Christians don't simply gather to exchange doctrinal affirmations. Rather, believers are called by God to get into each other's lives. We are family, for better or for worse, and we need to connect with each other.

Community is not built through sitting in the same building and singing the same songs. It is forged in the fires of life. When we know each other deeply — the good, the bad, and the ugly — community is experienced. Community grows when we learn to rejoice with one another, celebrating life. Roots grow deep when we know we are loved by others and are free to extend love to them as well. Finally, community deepens and is built when we commit to serve each other and let others serve us. This process of doing ministry and humbly receiving the ministry of others is critical for healthy community life.

Build Community Through Knowing and Being Known

We all long to know others deeply and to be fully known by them. Although we might run from this level of intimacy at times, we all want to have people in our lives who trust us enough to disclose the deep and tender parts of themselves. In turn, we want to reveal some of our feelings, expressing them freely to people we trust.

The first section of each of these six studies creates a place for deep knowing and being known. Through serious reflection on the truth of Scripture, you will be invited to communicate parts of your heart and life with your small group members. You might even discover yourself opening parts of your heart that you have thus far kept hidden. The Bible study and discussion questions do not encourage surface conversation. The only way to go deep in knowing others and being known by them is to dig deep, and this takes work. Knowing others also takes trust — that you will honor each other and respect each other's confidences.

Build Community Through Celebrating and Being Celebrated

If you have not had a good blush recently, read a short book in the Bible called Song of Songs. It's a record of a bride and groom writing poetic and romantic love letters to each other. They are freely celebrating every conceivable aspect of each other's personality, character, and physical appearance. At one point the groom says, "You have made my heart beat fast with a single glance from your eyes." Song of Songs is a reckless celebration of life, love, and all that is good.

We need to recapture the joy and freedom of celebration. In every session of this study, your group will commit to celebrate together. Although there are many ways to express joy, we will let our expression of celebration come through prayer. In each session you will take time to come before the God of joy and celebrate who he is and what he is doing. You will also have opportunity to celebrate what God is doing in your life and the lives of those who are a part of your small group. You will become a community of affirmation, celebration, and joy through your prayer time together.

You will need to be sensitive during this time of prayer together. Not everyone feels comfortable praying with a group of people. Be aware that each person is starting at a different place in their freedom to pray in a group, so be patient. Seek to promote a warm and welcoming atmosphere where each person can stretch a little and learn what it means to be a community that celebrates with God in the center.

Build Community Through Loving and Being Loved

Unless we are exchanging deeply committed levels of love with a few people, we will die slowly on the inside. This is precisely why so many people feel almost nothing at all. If we don't learn to exchange love with family and friends, we will eventually grow numb and no longer believe love is even a possibility. This is not God's plan. He hungers for us to be loved and to give love to others. As a matter of fact, he wants this for us even more than we want it for ourselves.

Every session in this study will address the area of loving and being loved. You will be challenged, in your personal life and as a small group, to be intentional and consistent about building loving relationships. You will get practical tools and be encouraged to set measurable goals for giving and receiving love.

Build Community Through Serving and Being Served

Community is about serving and humbly allowing others to serve you. The single most stirring example of this is recorded in John 13, where Jesus takes the position of the lowest servant and washes the feet of his followers. He gives them a powerful example and then calls them to follow. Servanthood is at the very core of community. To sustain deep relationships over a long period of time, there must be humility and a willingness to serve each other.

At the close of each session will be a clear challenge to servanthood. As a group, and as individual followers of Christ, you will discover that community is built through serving others. You will also find that your own small group members will grow in their ability to extend service to your life.

Bible Study Basics

To get the most out of this study, you will need to prepare and participate. Here are some guidelines to help you.

Preparing for the Study

1. If possible, even if you are not the leader, look over each session before you meet, read the Bible passages, and answer the questions. The more you are prepared, the more you will gain from the study.
2. Begin your preparation with prayer. Ask God to help you understand the passage and apply it to your life.
3. A good modern translation, such as the New International Version, Today's New International Version, the New American Standard Bible, or the New Revised Standard Version, will give you the most help. Questions in this guide are based on the New International Version.
4. Read and reread the passages. You must know what the passage says before you can understand what it means and how it applies to you.
5. Write your answers in the spaces provided in the study guide. This will help you participate more fully in the discussion and will also help you personalize what you are learning.
6. Keep a Bible dictionary handy to look up unfamiliar words, names, or places.

Participating in the Study

1. Be willing to join in the discussion. The leader of the group will not be lecturing but will encourage people to discuss what they have learned in the passage. Plan to share what God has taught you during your preparation time.
2. Stick to the passages being studied. Base your answers on the verses being discussed rather than on outside authorities such as commentaries or your favorite author or speaker.

3. Try to be sensitive to the other members of the group. Listen attentively when they speak, and be affirming whenever you can. This will encourage more hesistant members of the group to participate.
4. Be careful not to dominate the discussion. By all means participate, but allow others to have equal time.
5. If you are a discussion leader or a participant who wants further insights, you will find additional comments in the Leader's Notes at the back of the book.

Luke: Lessons from Jesus

Studying the life of Jesus is like looking at a diamond. There are many facets to a diamond and as you observe it from different angles, you get various perspectives on its beauty. If a person reads any of the four Gospels (Matthew, Mark, Luke, or John), they discover that Jesus lived a complex and multifaceted life.

Jesus was a miracle worker. He healed the blind, lame, and leprous. With a word or the touch of his hand, countless people experienced miraculous physical healing. He also calmed stormy seas, multiplied fish and bread, and walked on the water. Jesus had power over the physical world. There is no question that signs and wonders happened everywhere Jesus went.

Even a casual reading of the Gospels reveals Jesus as a revolutionary, constantly confronting the status quo. The religious leaders accused Jesus of not following their Sabbath laws, of failing to adhere to their cleansing rituals, and of daring to share meals with sinners and tax collectors (the social outcasts of the day). The political leaders watched him closely because they viewed him as a rival king who just might incite the crowds to rise up and overturn Roman rule.

But there was yet another side to Jesus—he was a pastor and a caring friend. People from every walk of life were drawn to him: adults and children, women and men, tax collectors and fishermen, religious leaders and sinners. They knew he loved them because he showed compassion to them.

Jesus was master of the spiritual world. With a single word the demons fled and possessed people were freed forever. He was tempted, face-to-face, by the devil and resisted all of the enticements the enemy presented. The angels of heaven ministered to him. Legions of angels were standing ready to follow his command. There is no question that Jesus was Lord over the spiritual powers in the cosmos.

Jesus also was a Rabbi, a mighty teacher who spoke powerful words of truth. His teaching was so profound that many of the people were in awe. They wondered how anyone could teach with such authority.

> Then he went down to Capernaum, a town in Galilee, and on the Sabbath began to teach the people. They were amazed at his teaching, because his message had authority. (Luke 4:31–32)

> All the people were amazed and said to each other, "What is this teaching? With authority and power he gives orders to evil spirits and they come out!" And the news about him spread throughout the surrounding area. (Luke 4:36–37)

> When Jesus had finished saying these things, the crowds were amazed at his teaching, because he taught as one who had authority, and not as their teachers of the law. (Matthew 7:28–29)

In this study we will focus on Jesus as a teacher of heavenly truth, a facet of his life that not only gives insight into the heart of God and the nature of his character, but provides right direction for our lives. The gospel of Luke devotes passage after passage to Jesus' teaching ministry; we will look at six topics that speak just as clearly to his followers today as they did two thousand years ago: the call to authentic humility, Christian discipleship, grace-filled evangelism, God's power to do miracles, the heart of servanthood, and the place of prayer. Each lesson from the lips of Jesus has the potential to transform our lives if we will listen and follow the words of the great Rabbi.

In the first century men and women were captivated by Jesus—they sat at his feet, were amazed by his teaching, and were forever changed by his truth. And the world was rocked.

Jesus is still the great teacher. Listen closely ... the Rabbi is speaking.

Christian Etiquette

LUKE 14:7–14; 18:9–14

Each culture has its own list of well-known and sometimes obscure rules of etiquette. One area of life that has a particularly high number of etiquette rules is mealtime. Consider: don't put your elbows on the table; pull a chair out for a woman; use certain pieces of silverware for certain courses; place a napkin on your lap; serve guests first; and chew with your mouth closed. When it comes to meals, some behaviors are deemed appropriate and others fall outside the boundaries of good manners.

Imagine dining at a nice restaurant when all of a sudden a man at the next table lets out a burp so loud it can be heard all the way in the kitchen. You would anticipate the whole restaurant falling silent as heads turn discreetly to identify who released this massive burst of gas. The glares and hushed conversations that would follow would be evidence that this was an epic breech of etiquette. Unless, of course, you are in a part of the world where a burp after the meal is understood to be a compliment to the cooks. In this case, no one would be offended and the cooks in the kitchen would smile with satisfaction as they heard the burp echoing through the restaurant.

The rules of etiquette change based on location and culture. On his web site, *The Sideroad*, Neil Payne offers guidelines on how to avoid dining faux pas and show good manners in different parts of the world. For instance, if you are having dinner in Germany, cut food with your fork and not your knife; this will tell the cook the food is tender. In Japan it is good manners to try a little of everything. In Turkey, asking for more food is taken as a compliment to the chef. In the Middle East you should tear your meat by holding it against the dish and tearing off a piece with your forefinger and thumb pressed together.

When it comes to wedding meals, certain rules of etiquette transcend time and many cultures. Imagine attending a wedding reception where up front, slighty elevated on risers, is a large head table set with special decorations, fine linen, fancy crystal, and the best china. As the reception begins, the guests enter and take their seats at round tables on the main floor, but two guests wander up to the empty head table and take the center seats. They are not in the wedding party. Everyone else in the room is sitting at the round tables with regular plates, plastic table covers, and ordinary silverware and glasses. They look at the two who have decided to take the places of honor and you can feel the tension in the air. Then the wedding party arrives. Can you guess what is going to happen next?

Making the Connection

1. Describe what you think will happen next in this wedding reception scenario.

Tell about a time when you, or someone else, broke a rule of etiquette (either knowingly or accidentally).

Knowing and Being Known

Read Luke 14:7 – 14

2. What are the rules of etiquette that come up in this passage?

What are some possible spiritual issues or lessons we find behind the rules of etiquette Jesus addresses?

The Danger of Presumption

Why is Jesus so concerned about protocol around tables and etiquette at meals? Is he really worried that one of his followers might get a wrong seat and then be asked to move to a different table? Is the Son of God all that concerned that one of his disciples would get the public recognition of being asked to come up to the head table after choosing to sit near the back of a banquet room? Is this really what Jesus is getting at with these rules of etiquette? Or, is there something deeper going on here?

As was often the case, Jesus was using an ordinary occurrence or life-situation as an opportunity to teach a profound spiritual lesson. If we take note of the setting of this story (Luke 14:1), we discover that Jesus was eating a meal in the house of a prominent religious leader. We also see that the people there were watching Jesus closely. What they did not notice was that Jesus was watching them too. He saw that as each guest entered the room they looked for the most prominent and best place to sit. They wanted to be noticed. They were focused on self-promotion. They were all about themselves. They were committing what can be called "the sin of presumption."

The issue was not the position of the seating chart, but the condition of their hearts. These guests wanted the best position and were ready to take it for themselves. They also had no concern for anyone else at the wedding banquet. Jesus was addressing a social presumption, but on a deeper level he was pointing out the problem with spiritual presumption. This comes when people become so obsessed with self that they actually believe they deserve a seat at every head table and recognition wherever they go.

Read Luke 14:7 – 10 and 18:9 – 14

3. How does each of these passages reveal a spiritual presumption of superiority?

How does God respond to this condition of the heart?

4. What are some of the ways people self-promote in our day and age, and how does this reflect a problem on a deep heart level?

5. Two signs that presumption is growing in our hearts are: (1) a feeling of being a little (or a lot) better than other people, and (2) an effort to constantly promote ourselves at the expense of others. What are some of the possible consequences of living with presumption in our hearts and actions in *one* of the following areas?

- Among siblings in a family system
- In a marriage
- In the workplace
- In the church
- In a neighborhood
- On an athletic team
- On a school campus

The Wisdom of Humility

I play a little game occasionally just to help keep my life in perspective. I don't do this out loud, but quietly, in my heart. I call it the "Where did you get that?" game. It goes something like this. I say, "Bill, it's time to make a list again. What do you have and where did you get it?" To start the game I begin to make a list:

- *My life*, where did I get this? It is a gift from God.
- The *breath I just drew in*, where do I get the air? God made it.
- Where did I get the *abilities* I have to teach and lead? These are gifts of the Spirit.
- How did I end up with such an extraordinary *wife*? Only God!
- I have *two healthy kids*, where did I receive such family blessings? From the hand of a loving God.
- The *church* I serve, how did I receive this privilege? Only from Jesus, the head of the church.

I can keep playing this game for a long time, and the answer to every one of my questions is always the same.

After I have played for a while I ask myself, "What do I have to brag about? What could I possible be haughty about? Why should I deserve a position of honor?" In these moments I am struck by the overwhelming reality that I am a recipient of God's grace in every way possible. I come to a place of healthy and profound humility because I not only get a clear picture of who God is and who I am, but I begin to see the people around me in a new light.

Read Luke 14:11 and Philippians 2:3 – 8

6. Make a list of ten things you have that you value (these can be abilities, material goods, relationships ... anything):

-
-

-
-

-
-

-
-

-
-

Take a moment on your own to play the "Where did I get it?" game. Look at each item on your list and honestly reflect on the source of all you have. Then discuss as a group what you noticed. Give an example of how God fits in when it comes to the source and origin of all you have.

How might this awareness impact the way you see yourself and the people around you?

7. Jesus gave the suggestion to sit in a low place and not grab the best seat at a wedding banquet. He called us to humility and became the best example in history of what choosing the way of humility looks like. What are some specific and practical ways people can take a lower seat and put others first?

What might happen if we actually took this invitation seriously and lived it out on a daily basis?

8. Consider a specific situation in life in which you believe God is calling you to humble yourself and take a lower seat.

What action could you take, and how can your group members encourage you and cheer you on as you grow in humility in this way?

Making Room for the Marginalized

We have seen that there is specific etiquette for guests at a banquet. Next, Jesus addresses another issue: the proper etiquette for hosting a lunch or dinner party. Who should be on the invitation list? Jesus' answer is radically countercultural, almost absurd. He says: Don't invite all the people you would normally invite; rather, invite the poor, hurting, and marginalized. He notes the people groups in his time that would have always been last (or never) on the guest list. Then he says, "These are the people you should invite first."

Remember the context of this whole teaching experience? Jesus is sharing a meal at the home of a prominent religious leader and has noticed that every guest had something to offer to the host. (Invitations to these dinners had a real give-and-take feel to them.) But again, Jesus is moving us past a physical example to a spiritual reality. God has a special place in his heart for the broken and marginalized in society. He cares about them and he wants us to care too. If we live by the world's system, we will never care for the outcasts because they have nothing to offer us in return. But if we live by God's system, we will care, love, and serve everyone … even those who don't care, love, or serve back.

Read Luke 14:12 – 14 and Zechariah 7:8 – 10

9. Passages in both the Old and New Testaments reveal a special place in God's heart for those who are poor, broken, abandoned, and living on the margins of society. Why do you think God feels so deeply for these groups of people?

Why does God call his followers to feel love and compassion for the marginalized and to take action on their behalf?

What can get in the way of us caring and taking the action that we should?

10. Just as there were specific groups of people who lived on the margins of society during Bible times, so there are today. Who are some of these groups of people now?

    How can we reach out to these people and extend an invitation into: our hearts, our homes, our church, our circle of friends?

11. Throughout history, the church (God's people gathered) has taken steps to care for the hurting of the world, whether providing food for the hungry or clothing for the poor, rebuilding houses for victims of a natural disaster, or caring for people battling various pandemic diseases. What are ways your church has tried to adopt the heart of God toward the marginalized and taken action to help the outcast?

    What possible future steps can your church or small group take to care for those who can never repay you, but who are deeply loved by God?

Celebrating and Being Celebrated

When we think of the outcast, the broken, the marginalized, and the "sinners" of society, we should think of ourselves. In God's sight, we are all broken without his grace. There was a time when we were separate from God. Reflect on this reality:

> Remember that at that time you were separate from Christ, excluded from citizenship in Israel and foreigners to the covenants of the promise, without hope and without God in the world. But now in Christ Jesus you who once were far away have been brought near through the blood of Christ. (Ephesians 2:12–13)

Take time as a group to pray, thanking God for what he has done to include you, embrace you, and invite you into his family. Then, pray that God will so fill your hearts that you are ready to love the outcasts of this world the way he loves you.

Loving and Being Loved

One way to keep your perspective right is to periodically remember that all you have is a gift from God. Put a weekly reminder in your calendar for the coming month to play the "Where did I get it?" game (see page 17), then be sure to follow through. If someone happens to notice your calendar notation and asks about it, explain how you are learning that all you have is a gift from God and that this knowledge brings both thankfulness and humility in how you relate to others.

Serving and Being Served

Take time as a small group to identify one way you can work together to serve a person or a group that has been marginalized.

Try to steer away from giving money or anything that feels more passive. Look instead for a ministry opportunity that will move you into action and get you in proximity and relationship with someone who has been marginalized.

Back to Basics

LUKE 14:25–33

There are times in life when the best possible course of action is going back to the basics, moments when the fundamentals and foundational issues need to be returned to center stage. The great Green Bay Packers football coach, Vince Lombardi, was famous for standing in the middle of his players with a football in hand and beginning a speech, "Gentlemen, this is a football." You can't get more basic than that. Some people have the ability to distill information down into its most essential elements. Here are a few more examples from Coach Lombardi:

Once you learn to quit, it becomes a habit.

If you'll not settle for anything less than your best, you will be amazed at what you can accomplish in your lives.

It's not whether you get knocked down, it's whether you get up.

If you aren't fired with enthusiasm, you'll be fired with enthusiasm.

Similarly, there were times in Jesus' ministry when he made a point of taking people back to the basics. In these moments he would speak with such precision and clarity that the people around him knew exactly what it meant to be his follower. In these moments people had to decide, "Am I really ready to follow Jesus?"

Making the Connection

1. Briefly make your own list of what you believe it means to follow Jesus. What are the top five or six things Jesus expects of those who call themselves a Christ follower?

How do you think Jesus would finish the following statement if he were sitting with your small group right now: One of the most important things I want to see my followers do today is ...

Knowing and Being Known

Read Luke 14:25 – 33

The Three "R's"

In the message recorded in Luke 14, Jesus gets back to the basics. At the start of the passage we read that large crowds were following him. Jesus was not always a big fan of crowds, knowing that many were coming to hear him teach only because it was the popular thing to do. In fact, whenever he clarified what it truly meant to follow him, many in the crowds left. And that's exactly what happened in this instance when Jesus addresses the three R's.

For many years Americans talked about the three R's (colloquially referred to as reading, 'riting, and 'rithmetic) as the basics of a solid education. Here in Luke Jesus spoke about the three R's that are basic to anyone who wants to be his follower. They deal with: relationships, responsibility, and resources. If we can get these right, we will be well on the way to growing into maturity as Christ followers.

2. What does Jesus teach about each of the following topics in this message:
   • Relationships (v. 26)

   • Responsibility (v. 27)

   • Resources (vv. 28–33)

   Imagine you were one of the people in the crowd who had just begun following this increasingly popular Rabbi. How might you have responded to these three challenges?

3. In your time as a follower of Christ, how has your faith in him impacted *one* of these areas:
   • How you see your relational life
   • What you are willing to sacrifice
   • How you view and use your resources

Relationships: Who's Number One?

The first "R" is relationships. In this passage Jesus says that unless we "hate" our family members and even our own life we can't follow him. These words bother a lot of people. The word "hate" really throws them for a loop. "Hate" here does not mean that we should dislike or have bad feelings toward our family. In other portions of the Bible we are instructed to love our spouse and children; in the Ten Commandments we are called to honor our parents; all through the Scriptures God teaches that we should love our brothers and sisters.

What Jesus means is this: if we are going to be his follower, we must understand that only one relationship in the entire universe demands our ultimate allegiance. Only one relationship can be absolutely preeminent in our life, and that is our relationship with Jesus Christ. Our love for him should be so pure and our devotion to him so passionate that all other relationships—spouse, children, parents, brothers, sisters, our closest friends—pale in comparison. For a fully devoted follower of Christ, our greatest priority is always God and the focus of our heart is Jesus. Nothing else comes close to comparing.

Read Luke 14:25–26 and Luke 8:19–21

4. What helps you keep Christ at the center of your life and the primary passion of your heart?

What are some of the things that can tend to creep in and try to take first place in your heart and life?

5. How can an inappropriate allegiance to another person get in the way of our following and obeying God?

What sacrifices might we have to make by choosing God's will instead of the wishes of another person?

6. As followers of Christ we are called to put Jesus before family members, friends, and every other relationship. If we hear this call and pursue God as our first passion, how might this impact *one* of the following:
   - Our ability to be a spouse who loves and serves faithfully
   - Our effectiveness in being a parent who points our children toward Jesus
   - Our capacity for honoring parents all the days of their lives
   - Our consistency in being a friend who gives godly encouragement and wisdom
   - Our passion for sharing the message of Jesus with people who are spiritually searching

Responsibility: Discovering My Part in God's Kingdom

The second "R" is responsibility. Jesus speaks these words on his way to Jerusalem where he will die on a cross and give his life for the world. This was his mission, his primary responsibility. Listen to his words: "For

28

God did not send his Son into the world to condemn the world, but to save the world through him" (John 3:17) and "For even the Son of Man did not come to be served, but to serve, and to give his life as a ransom for many" (Mark 10:45). Jesus took his calling very seriously.

Every believer in Jesus, every true disciple, will be given a mission, a calling, a responsibility that has kingdom implications. Jesus carried a cross for us and he calls us to carry the cross for his sake. Jesus saw the crowds and wanted them to know that following him would cost something … it would cost everything.

Read Luke 14:27 and Luke 9:23 – 27

7. Following Jesus involves sacrifice. The picture of carrying the cross would have brought vivid images to first-century believers. They knew what a brutal and humiliating experience it was to be executed on a cross. Think about three specific realities that would come with carrying a cross. How have you experienced these as you have walked with Jesus?

   • The *weight* of the cross — What burdens and loads has God called you to lift as you follow Jesus?

   • The *seriousness* of the cross — How has following Jesus brought a sobriety about the spiritual needs and realities in our world?

   • The *pain* of the cross — In what ways have you endured pain, sorrow, or struggle because you have willingly followed Jesus?

8. Part of the responsibility of carrying the cross is putting down some things that we can't keep carrying if we are going to take up the cross. As a follower of Christ, what are some of the things Jesus has called you to put down so you can follow him fully?

Picking up the cross is about taking the responsibilities God places on your life. What are some responsibilities you live with that you would have never had if you were not a follower of Christ?

Resources: Be Ready to Relinquish Them

The third and final "R" in this message is about how we handle our resources. Jesus calls his followers to take a serious account of all we have. Once we acknowledge our every possession, we are to come to his throne and lay them all down. That's right ... everything. This is part of discipleship.

It is important to note that the Bible is not teaching that possession of material goods is wrong or sinful. Jesus is not saying that every one of his followers should sell all they have and live in a commune. When Jesus says to "give up" everything he is calling us to relinquish it all to his purposes and plan. He calls us to be good stewards of what he places in our care. We are to love God, not the stuff of this world. If we can learn to use resources for God's kingdom and refuse to let money and possessions become a love in our life, we are well down the road to being his disciples.

Read Luke 14:28 – 33; Luke 16:13; I Timothy 6:10; and Hebrews 13:5

9. What are some of the indicators that we might still be in love with money and material things?

Why is the love of money such a powerful force in our society and lives?

10. Do you see some hope-filled signs that God is setting you free from the love of money, that the grip and power of possessions is being broken in your life? What are they?

11. What are you trying to do to strike a healthy and Christ-honoring balance between owning possessions and letting your possessions own you?

How does generosity and giving factor into creating this balanced lifestyle?

Celebrating and Being Celebrated

The first "R" is about keeping our relationship with God first ... above all human relationships. Meditate on the greatness of God's love for you. Think about all he has done, and continues to do. Then, spend time as a group thanking God for:

- His great love
- His desire to be in a relationship with you
- Opening the way to restored intimacy through the sacrifice of Jesus
- All of his provisions

Loving and Being Loved

Sometimes we try to de-cross the cross. We can be tempted to want Jesus but not want to bear his cross. Take time in the coming week to meet with Jesus and make a fresh commitment to follow him, no matter what the cost. You might want to pray, "Lord, you bled and died on a cross. I am ready to take up your cross each day. I know it will be painful at times. I am sure it will get heavy. I am aware that following you is serious business. I will carry whatever weight you want me to carry. Here is my life. Take me. Use me." Give God the one gift no one else in all the world can give him ... your devotion, your life, and your heart.

Serving and Being Served

As we bear the cross of Jesus we hear his call to service. Every follower of Christ is filled with the Holy Spirit and gifted for ministry. Unfortunately, many people in the local church are much more comfortable receiving than giving when it comes to ministry. We are often uncomfortable with the idea of offering our resources for God's work. Commit to a new level of service by offering God two things in response to what he asks of you. First, devote yourself to the responsibility of ministry. Find some way you can serve in your church or community. Second, offer your resources to be used for God's purposes in this world. Hold nothing back.

Lessons from Lazarus

LUKE 16:19-31

There are certain times in life when people become thoughtful, introspective, and naturally ponder the purpose and meaning of life. One such time is when we stand next to a casket. Have you been there? It could be a funeral, a visitation, or a graveside service, but something about these moments takes us to an instant place of sober reflection.

Jesus told all kinds of stories and taught countless lessons. Often the images he used were cheerful and uplifting: a shepherd who finds his lost sheep, lilies of the field, birds of the air, a good and generous Samaritan.

Jesus also addressed hard truths through stories. One day he told a story about two funerals. But Jesus did something no one else could do: he pulled back the veil of eternity and gave a glance into the afterlife. Through the story of the rich man and Lazarus, Jesus not only invites us to reflect on the reality of death, but he also helps us learn from what happens after this life ends.

In this session we stand at a gravesite. There are two headstones. One says "The Rich Man" and the other says "Lazarus." Each one lived, died, and has crossed over into eternity. Their lives were dramatically dissimilar but their eternities are even more different. They both have a story to tell. If we listen, it could impact our life and our eternity.

Making the Connection

1. Why do graveside experiences prompt such deep reflection and sober evaluation of life?

Tell about a time you attended a funeral, stood by a graveside, or lost a person you cared about. How did reflecting on their passing impact your life?

Knowing and Being Known

Read Luke 16:19–31

2. How were the rich man and Lazarus different in life?

How were they different in death?

3. What do you learn about *one* of the following topics as you read this story?
   - The potential impact of riches on our attitudes and actions
   - The reality and nature of heaven and hell
   - The motivation to share the message of salvation in Jesus

Potential Pitfalls of Wealth

One lesson Jesus is teaching in this story is that affluence can breed excess and insensitivity. Jesus is not saying that it is wrong to have material things. But the attitude of the rich man in the story is heartbreaking. A poor beggar named Lazarus lived right outside the rich man's house and the rich man had to walk past him, almost step over his body, on a daily basis. Lazarus was sick and starving. To make things worse, the dogs came and licked his sores. Yet the rich man never seemed to notice nor did he ever stop to help. He had plenty he could have shared, but the truth is, he did not care.

Sadly, one of the attitudes that can accompany affluence is the expectation and demand for even more wealth. Affluent people can begin to think they deserve the best things in life. It can be a slow and subtle progression, but over time they can become blind to the people around them who have profound needs. The more they focus on what they have and all they want, the less they think about those who have less ... the people they could help and serve.

Read Luke 16:19 – 21; Luke 12:16 – 21; and James 1:17

4. How does God feel about those who hoard what they have and become so insensitive that they don't notice or come to the aid of those in need around them?

5. How have you seen increasing wealth create a growing sense of entitlement?

How can understanding James 1:17 help us overcome a self-centered attitude of entitlement?

6. It would seem that people who have more material resources naturally would be more generous. But the teaching of Jesus and real-life experience teach us that this is not always the case. How can an increase of wealth and the accumulation of material things actually desensitize us to the needs of the poor and the broken in the world?

What can help us open our eyes, heart, and hands to the needy in our world?

The Reality of Heaven and Hell

This story teaches a sobering lesson that many people today do not want to face: there is a real heaven, a real hell, and real people will spend eternity in one place or the other. C. S. Lewis once said, "You have never met a mere mortal." In other words, every person you meet will live forever. The question is, where will they spend eternity?

We don't know exactly what heaven and hell will be like. But the Bible paints enough pictures to assure us that heaven is eternal joy and communion with God and hell is eternal torment and separation from God. That should be enough to wake us up to the reality that people need to hear the message of God's grace in Jesus Christ.

A growing number of people today want to revise the Bible to edit out things they don't like. Certainly a belief in hell is on that list. Some people who call themselves Christians try to argue that the Bible does not teach the existence of hell. They embrace what is called "universalism," the belief that everyone will end up in heaven. The dilemma is that the Bible does not support this man-made belief. We may not like the concept of hell, but followers of Christ don't have the luxury of removing biblical truth just because it makes us uncomfortable.

Read Luke 16:22 – 28; Luke 23:40 – 43; and Romans 8:18

7. How can embracing the biblical teaching of heaven give us hope and strength in the challenging times of life?

8. What would you say to a person who declares: "I can't believe in a real hell because God is loving and would never judge or punish people"?

How can believing in a real heaven and a real hell stir our hearts to share the gospel and love of Jesus with people who are still far from God?

Share the Gospel While You Can

The rich man became an evangelist once he was in hell. At this point he saw the whole spiritual reality unfold. No one had to tell him that heaven and hell were real. But it was too late. He learned that there is a chasm between heaven and hell and no one passes back and forth. Now the rich man wanted to go back and warn his family, but it was too late. What a lesson for followers of Christ. We have this life, and this life only, to reach out to spiritual seekers. We have one life to live and one of our passionate pursuits should be sharing the amazing message of God's love found in Jesus Christ alone.

We also have only one life to show compassion, feed the poor, and care for those who are broken. If the rich man could have done it all over, he might have noticed the needs of Lazarus and offered some food and care.

You might have the spiritual gift of evangelism, and you might not. But every follower of Christ is called to "be prepared to give an answer to everyone who asks you to give the reason for the hope you have" (1 Peter 3:15). Jesus said that we are to be his light in this world of darkness (Matthew 5:14 – 16). The apostle Paul invited us to become fools for Jesus (1 Corinthians 1:18 – 25). In other words, every Christ follower is expected to get involved in the work of bringing the message of salvation to our lost and broken world through our words and through Christ-honoring acts of compassion.

Read Luke 16:27 – 31; Luke 24:45 – 49; and 1 Corinthians 1:20 – 25

9. If the rich man in this story could stand up for ten minutes in your church some weekend and speak to the people gathered there, what do you think he would say?

10. Why does our world see the message of Jesus as foolishness and those who share the gospel as fools?

Tell about a time you or someone you know had the privilege of being a "fool for Jesus" as the message of grace was shared.

11. What motivates you to share the love and message of Jesus with people who are still far from God?

Who is one person God has placed in your life that needs to come to faith in Jesus, and how does God want to use you as a witness in the life of this person?

Celebrating and Being Celebrated

God did not have to make a way for people to experience forgiveness and grace. He could have left us in our sin. But, in his great love, God sent his only Son to open the door to heaven. All who have received God's grace in Jesus have the assurance that heaven will be their eternal home. Take time as a group to offer prayers of praise and celebration for:

- The amazing love of God that allowed him to offer his Son as the payment for our sins
- The grace of Jesus that covers our sins
- The reality of heaven and the hope that exists for all who have faith in Jesus
- The privilege we have to share the good news of Jesus with those who are lost

Loving and Being Loved

If heaven and hell are real, one of the greatest acts of love we could ever extend is sharing the message of grace found in Jesus Christ alone. If we love a friend, neighbor, colleague at work, or family member, we will want them to spend this life and eternity in fellowship with God. This means entering into God's plan for reaching the world.

Take time to write down the names of a few people in your life who have not yet started a relationship with God the Father through Jesus his Son.

-
-
-

Commit to pray for some of the following things in the coming month:

- Ask for the Holy Spirit to soften the hearts of the people on your list to the love and message of Jesus.
- Pray for yourself as you seek to serve, love, and communicate the gospel to these people.
- Pray for your church to be a place of love and grace where you could invite spiritual seekers.
- Surrender your life to God's will and let God know you are willing to be a "fool" for him if that is what it takes to reach people with the message of Christ.

Serving and Being Served

God wants to see his whole church equipped to share the good news of Jesus and to be passionate about this calling. Consider serving your congregation by introducing a class or churchwide learning experience on the topic of personal evangelism. Two practical tools for inspiring and equipping followers of Christ for outreach are: *Becoming a Contagious Christian* and *Just Walk Across the Room*. More details for these training tools can be found on the Zondervan website: www.zondervan.com.

How to Receive a Miracle

LUKE 17:11–19

What do you do when you are faced with a problem you cannot solve?

Where do you go when you experience a disappointment you cannot bear?

To whom do you cry when it feels like life is caving in all around you?

Where do you turn when a relationship is strained and on the verge of falling apart?

When you come to the end of your rope, your resources, and your abilities, what do you do?

The truth is that all of us hit points in our lives when we need a miracle. Sometimes these miracles are the big, amazing, nature-bending moments of God's intervention. God has performed all kinds of miracles through history. He has raised the dead, parted seas, rained bread from heaven, given sight to the blind, calmed storms, driven out demons, and fed thousands of people with a few loaves and fishes. Miracles are no problem for God.

But some people define a "miracle" too narrowly. Unless a stone is rolling away from a tomb, the crippled are walking, or the sun stops in the sky, to them it is not a miracle. In this session we will look at the reality that God still does miracles: some of them are nature-breaking invasions of his power, but others are the supernatural interventions of a loving God in our daily lives. God still can and does both kinds of miracles.

God wants to do miracles, both large and small, in each of our lives. If you have need of God's supernatural intervention to meet a need in your life, you are looking for a miracle. There are times when we face challenges or trials in the workplace and we know the only way we will make it through is with God's power ... we need a miracle. There are marriages that are so damaged that only a miracle of God will put the pieces back together. There are financial circumstances that look so hopeless that without a powerful intervention of God there is no way out. Some face emotional struggles that hang like a dark cloud and, without a miracle, no hope appears on the horizon. No matter what we face today, we need to be assured of the fact that God can, and still does, perform miracles!

Making the Connection

1. Describe a time you needed a powerful intervention of God in some area of your life and he showed up in a miraculous way and carried you through.

What is one miracle you need in your life right now, and how can your group members pray with you for this miracle?

Knowing and Being Known

Read Luke 17:11 – 19
2. What was Jesus' part in this miracle involving the lepers?

What was the lepers' part in receiving a miracle from God?

Cry Out for God's Help

The first step in receiving a miracle is coming to God with our need and crying out for help. In this passage we meet ten men who had leprosy, a very real need. They were sick, they were outcasts, and they wanted to be healed. There is not one person who walks this earth who does not have needs, but the question is, will we cry out to God for help? The lepers in the story expressed their need to Jesus—they cried out for help.

It seems strange, but there are people who need a miraculous intervention of God in their life, but they don't ask for his help. Some people are too busy complaining about their situation. It almost seems they like having something to whine about, preferring to focus on their problems instead of God's possible solutions. Others have given up on life and faith. They won't ask God for help because they think they are in a hopeless situation. These people would love to see their life change, but they are sure that it never will. There are even people who are committed to figuring out and fixing their own problems. They want to be strong and self-sufficient so they won't ask anyone, not even God, for help.

Read Luke 17:11 – 13 and Luke 11:9 – 10

3. Many things can keep people from crying out to God for help. Tell about how you have seen people fail to ask for God's miraculous intervention for *one* of the following reasons:
   - Because they seem to like complaining about how hard their life is
   - Because they have become hopeless and discouraged
   - Because they are committed to figuring things out on their own, without God's help
   - Because they have asked for help in the past and do not feel God acted the way they wanted

- Because their theology says that God does not intervene in our daily lives
- Because they believe they are unworthy of God's help and miraculous love

What do you think Jesus would say to this person about their reason for not crying out for God's help?

4. What can get in the way of you asking God for help and a miraculous intervention in your life?

What needs to happen for you to come to a place where you will really cry out, in faith, for God's power to be released in your life today?

Receive God's Direction

The second essential ingredient for receiving a miracle is receiving direction from above. When the lepers cried out, Jesus gave them clear and specific directions: "Go, show yourselves to the priests." This might not seem like a big deal to us today, but these men had personal history with the priests. As was the custom, when each of them had begun to show signs of leprosy they would have been brought to the priests to have their skin examined. In each case, a priest had declared them "unclean."

It was the words of a priest that had consigned them to a leper colony on the outskirts of society. It was a priest who had taught them that whenever they approached another person they had to shout out the word, "Unclean!" so people could avoid them. The priests were so concerned about lepers that any contact, no matter how incidental (including having the shadow of a leper touch them), would make them ceremonially unclean.

Now Jesus tells these ten men, "Go show yourselves to the priests." At this point, they were still covered with leprosy. Their condition was likely much worse than when a priest first declared them "unclean" and banished them from the city. You can almost hear the lepers thinking, "You mock us. Don't you think we have experienced enough humiliation? Now you are asking us to walk all the way back into the city shouting 'unclean' every step of the way. Then you want us to visit the priests and hear them explain that we are still not welcome." What Jesus asked of these men would demand courage and faith.

Read Luke 17:14

5. Often when we ask God for a miracle he will call us to enter into the process in some tangible way. He calls us to do something, to take a step of faith. Part of the miracle is that we move into action. Tell about a time you knew God was calling you to take a step of faith that you were reluctant to take.

What happened when you took that step and followed God's leading in that situation?

6. When we feel a prompting to take a step of faith, there are many ways we can confirm that it is God who is leading us. Talk as a group about how some of these confirmations can help give confidence and wisdom as you follow God's leading:
   - Testing every prompting and leading against the teaching of the Bible
   - Gaining wisdom from mature and godly followers of Christ
   - Looking back through your life and the lives of other believers to determine if this leading is consistent with God's work in the past
   - Looking back through the history of the church to see that the leading you feel has been experienced by other followers of Christ
   - Other confirmations you find helpful ...

Step Out in Faith

Many followers of Christ have a need and cry out to God for help. They receive direction from him and have it confirmed through the teaching of Scripture. But, in many cases, the miracle dies right there because they refuse to take the steps necessary to follow God.

The ten lepers could have easily stopped right here in the process. They had received the direction, "Go, show yourselves to the priest." It sounded silly, illogical, distasteful, and even humiliating. Why would they ask for another examination of their skin when they could look at their own hands, arms, and legs and see that they were covered with leprosy? Yet, what we read next is one of the greatest phrases in all of Scripture: "And as they went, they were cleansed." Their faith was demonstrated by taking action on the direction that came from heaven.

One of the greatest needs for Christ followers today is to be able to quietly wait on the Lord so that we can ascertain his direction and leading. Another equally important need is for Christians to have enough faith to say, "I don't care how silly the direction sounds, how illogical it might be. By faith I am going to take the step that God asks me to take." When we can do this with confidence, we are on our way to experiencing God's miracles.

Read Luke 17:14

7. What is the relationship between God's power to do miracles and our willingness to take the steps he calls us to take?

Respond to this statement: *All sorts of miracles are never experienced because Christ followers refuse to take the steps of faith God calls them to take.*

8. What step of faith has God been calling you to take, but you have been standing still instead of moving forward?

How can your group members pray for you, encourage you forward, and keep you accountable to take this step of faith?

Express Thanksgiving

What happens when you receive a miracle? What do you do when God supernaturally intervenes and gives a solution, heals a relationship, or provides something you desperately need? How *should* you respond?

The ten lepers in this story paint a vivid picture for us. Nine of them were healed as they journeyed and kept right on the road to the city, straight to the priests to get their declaration of cleansing. Who could blame them? This was their ticket back to society, back to a life they had barely dreamed they would experience again. But one of the lepers, upon discovering his skin miraculously restored, did an about-face to return to Jesus, giving loud thanks and praise to God as he went. What an example!

Read Luke 17:15 – 19

9. How is it that ten people could experience the same miraculous healing but respond in such different ways?

10. What are some of the things that can cause us to be like the nine lepers and miss opportunities to give praise and thanks to God?

11. What helps you stay aware of God's goodness and work in your life so that you are quick to draw near to him and give thanks?

Celebrating and Being Celebrated

We have all experienced times when God's miraculous power invaded and we have seen him do great things for us or for someone we love. Offer prayers of thanksgiving and praise for the great things God has done in your life. Be like the one leper who came back praising God with a loud voice. As a group, express prayers of deep gratitude and thanks to God for his miracles.

Loving and Being Loved

One of the best ways we can grow in love is receiving God's care through other people. Identify a couple of people in your life who are mature in faith and whom you trust deeply. Use them as a sounding board when you are seeking wisdom in your life direction. Specifically, if you feel God is calling you to specific action, ask for these people to pray and share their insights. Their insights will help you discern when you are hearing God's voice and leading.

Serving and Being Served

God deserves our praise. When we are alone and God does something powerful, we can lift our voice in adoration. But we are also called to lift up praise when we gather together. One of the best ways we can serve the people around us is modeling a heart filled with thankful praise. When God has set us free, given us guidance, or restored us in places of brokenness, we should share these stories of God's miraculous presence and power. What miraculous work has God accomplished in your life? Take time this week to share this story with someone else. Tell of God's amazing power and let your story bring hope and inspiration to others.

Becoming a Servant

LUKE 17:7–10; 12:35–40

To say that Jesus was countercultural would be an understatement of epic proportions. Throughout his life and ministry Jesus questioned the conventional wisdom of his day, cultural and religious norms that everyone took for granted. His teaching stretched people to see life through new lenses, to the point that they did not quite know how to respond. Consider just a few of the radical teachings of Jesus:

> Indeed there are those who are last who will be first, and first who will be last. (Luke 13:30)

> For whoever wants to save his life will lose it, but whoever loses his life for me will save it. (Luke 9:24)

> You have heard that it was said, "Love your neighbor and hate your enemy." But I tell you: Love your enemies and pray for those who persecute you, that you may be sons of your Father in heaven. (Matthew 5:43–45)

One of the most striking ways that Jesus called his followers to a revolutionary lifestyle was his teaching on servanthood. Over and over Jesus taught and modeled a life of service.

> Sitting down, Jesus called the Twelve and said, "If anyone wants to be first, he must be the very last, and the servant of all." (Mark 9:35)

After washing the feet of the disciples, a dramatic act of service, Jesus said:

You call me "Teacher" and "Lord," and rightly so, for that is what I am. Now that I, your Lord and Teacher, have washed your feet, you also should wash one another's feet. I have set you an example that you should do as I have done for you. (John 13:13–15)

In all four Gospels this message rings out loud and clear. Those who call themselves followers of Jesus are to live the way he did, embracing service as a lifestyle, not just as an occasional recreational activity. Jesus did not simply serve, he lived as a servant. From his humble birth in a stable to his death on a cross between two common criminals, Jesus gave us a picture of what it looks like to serve with humble joy.

Making the Connection

1. Tell about a person in your life who has modeled humble and joyful service as part of who they are.

How have you seen Jesus alive and working through this person?

Read Luke 17:7 – 10 and Luke 12:35 – 40

2. What are some of the ways Jesus modeled the heart and life of a servant?

How is Jesus continuing to serve us — his followers and the church — even today?

3. What do you learn from these two passages about the right attitude and actions of those who follow Christ as servants?

Wrong Motives for Serving

It would be nice to think that everyone who serves does so with healthy motives, but such is not always the case. It is important for us to examine our hearts to make sure we are not serving with the wrong motives.

Some people serve as *an effort to gain God's favor and love.* They believe that if they offer an occasional humanitarian gesture or engage in a few religious endeavors they will get a few points with "the Big Guy in the Sky" and that he will look kindly on them at judgment day.

Some people serve *for human applause.* Wanting recognition and praise from a peer group, they look for things they can do that people will notice and applaud.

Some people serve *for "self-actualization."* Their driving force and goal is to bolster a sense of positive self-esteem. They want to feel good about themselves, to believe they are worthwhile and valuable persons. So they serve others, but in reality, they are being self-serving.

Many people serve in an effort *to appease their sense of shame and guilt.* They might have wronged people in the past and their service is a way of paying penance. They might be wealthy and by helping others on occasion they feel justified living in opulence. Or, they might just be dealing with deep feelings of guilt and they feel better when they do some act of service to help another person.

God loves when we serve, and he understands that our motives are rarely pure as the driven snow. But he wants us to come to a place where we are motivated to serve because we have experienced his love and desire to share it with others.

Read Luke 17:7 – 10 and Acts 20:22 – 24

4. How can serving spin in unhealthy directions when it is motivated by:
   - An effort to get God's love?
   - A need to gain the praise of people?
   - A desire to attain personal fulfillment?
   - An effort to cover our shame and guilt?

5. What are some of the good, healthy, and godly motivations for a follower of Christ to serve?

How can the right motivation shape our service and help us serve for a lifetime?

6. Describe the times you felt you were most naturally and passionately serving for the sake of Jesus. What was happening in your heart, and what motivated you in these times of service?

Rendering Service or Becoming a Servant?

In his book, *Celebration of Discipline*, Richard Foster says, "There is a tremendous difference between rendering service and becoming a servant." Many Christ followers are willing, from time to time, to render service. It can be exciting to go on a mission trip for a week, teach a youth class for a couple of months, serve at a food pantry for a Saturday, or help a neighbor in a moment of need. Most of us are fine with offering an act of service on occasion. But that is dramatically different than becoming a servant.

Rendering service is generally about a short-term foray into the world of serving, done when it's convenient, isn't too demanding, doesn't cramp our style, and if we like the people we are working with. Most Christ followers are willing to serve like this ... once in a while. But *becoming a servant* gets to the very core of our heart and identity. It is not so much about a project or activity, but a disposition of our soul. When we become a servant, all of our actions flow out of this identity.

Read Philippians 2:3 – 8 and John 13:2 – 17

7. How did Jesus become a servant rather than just offering acts of service?

Once Jesus was a servant, how did his actions grow out of this identity?

8. Why is it easier to render acts of service rather than become a servant?

9. If you actually see your core identity as being a servant, how could this impact *one* of the following:
   - How you feel and respond when someone asks you to help with a task that seems "below you"
   - How you respond when you have served faithfully and no one says, "Thank you"
   - How you treat people who have been unkind or selfish toward you
   - How you serve when no one is around and no one will ever know

Natural and Enthusiastic Servants

The desire to extend humble service to others happens when our eyes and hearts are fixed on Jesus. It just begins to grow from the inside out. When we come to the manger and see the Creator and God of the universe reduced to an infant and born in the stench of a stable, we cannot help but be affected. When we see Jesus, the Lord of glory, stooping down to wash the dirt off his disciples' feet, something in us breaks. We realize that if we had been at that table, Jesus would have washed our feet too (remember, Judas was there and Jesus washed his feet). When we look up at a Roman cross and see the sinless Son of God nailed there, taking the judgment we deserved, the whole world looks different.

We know we are growing into Christ-honoring servants when service comes naturally and with heartfelt enthusiasm. As the Spirit of Jesus lives in our hearts, we find serving is not a chore, a job, or a religious duty but a joy and a passion, a way to identify with our Savior. And, as we serve, we have a profound sense that Jesus takes delight as we reflect his servant-presence in the world.

Read Luke 12:35 – 40

10. How does this passage paint a picture of a person who is ready to serve at all times?

What does it mean to "Be dressed, ready for service," and to "keep your lamps burning"?

11. What is an area of service you know God has called you to enter into? (You might already be serving in this area or just aware that God is calling you to serve.)

How can your group members pray for you and encourage you to serve with enthusiasm and joy in this place of Christlike service?

Celebrating and Being Celebrated

Spend time as a group thanking God for his example of humble and passionate service revealed in Jesus. Pray through the life of Jesus as you do this:

- For the incarnation and the way he emptied himself and left heaven for you
- For his birth in a manger
- For a life of ministry and humble service for sinful people
- For giving his life on the cross for your sins
- For the way he sent the Holy Spirit to dwell in you
- For the way he serves you today by protecting, granting power, interceding for you, and so much more

Loving and Being Loved

We all have people in our lives who have modeled what it looks like to be a godly and humble servant. When you watch them there is no sense that serving is a chore or a project; it is just what they do. These people have revealed the presence of Jesus as they have served us. If such a person comes to mind right now, take time to write them a note expressing how God has used them to teach you what it looks like to be a servant. Thank this person for their ministry to you.

Serving and Being Served

Take time in the coming week for a service checkup. Use this session to guide you through three areas of personal evaluation.

1. Review the four wrong motives for serving (see page 54). Do any of these motives drive you? If so, pray for a new attitude and Christ-centered motives for serving.
2. Examine yourself during the week to identify if you are a person who offers occasional acts of service, or if you are becoming a real servant. The truth is, none of us has perfected a servantlike heart. The key is that we are moving away from simply rendering service and moving toward being servants. Where are you on this journey?
3. Are you growing more enthusiastic about serving, and is it flowing naturally from you? Pray that this will happen in growing measure.

Keep Praying

LUKE 18:1–8

We pray, and we pray, then we pray some more. With earnestness and fervency we lift up our hearts and the needs we carry so deep within us. We cry out in what feels like a ceaseless chorus of supplication as we ask God to hear, to answer, and to intervene. Then, after what feels like endless petition and knocking on the door of heaven, we give up. We tried and it did not work. We were faithful to do our part in prayer every single day for what felt like an eternity ... well, it was six days in a row. But, why keep asking when it is clear that God is not going to answer.

Have you ever hit a wall in prayer? If you have, you are not alone. Followers of Christ have been dealing with the motivation for prayer for about two thousand years. For many Christians it is difficult to stay fired up for prayer over the long haul. Why is this? Why don't many of Christ's followers pray more? I believe one big answer is that many people stop praying because they don't think they get their prayers answered enough.

When we pray and receive a dramatic response from heaven, we are motivated to pray more. We think, "God took care of that need, I'll move to the next item on my list." The more answers we get, the more we want to pray. But it works the other way too. If we don't get an answer to a particular prayer, what do we conclude? *Prayer doesn't work. God isn't listening. There is an obstacle I can't figure out. Something's wrong with me. Prayers are answered in other people's lives, but not in mine.* When we think this way, we have a tendency to pray less and lose heart. We become faint in our prayers.

Making the Connection

1. What motivates you and keeps you passionate about prayer?

   What discourages you from praying and causes you to shy away from regular and faith-filled prayer?

Knowing and Being Known

Read Luke 18:1 – 8

2. Through the years many people have been confused by this story because they have tried to read it as an allegory. In other words, they try to create a one-to-one correspondence between each element of the story and a spiritual reality. As an exercise in biblical interpretation, reread this parable and draw out the natural and logical conclusions you arrive at if you interpret the judge as God and the widow as us. Just a little warning: you won't like most of the answers.

   If the judge in this story represents God (the recipient of our prayers):

   How does God feel about people?

Why does God answer prayer?

If the widow represents praying Christians:
How do we get what we want from God?

How does God view us when we pray?

3. The main point of this parable is expressed clearly in the first verse. How does the parable reinforce this central message?

Contrast #1: God Is Not Like the Judge

In this parable we meet a desperate widow who is helpless, penniless, without connections or clout. What a sad beginning. We also meet a despicable judge who is cold to God and heartless toward people. The problem is that the only way this woman will get justice is if the judge grants it, and he couldn't care less! So, what does she do? She bugs this guy so much that he gives her what she wants because he is sick of her. Is this an accurate picture of prayer? Is this the message of Jesus? You might conclude … if you ever want anything from God you will have to bug him until he is so tired of you that he answers your prayer just so you will go away! That is *not* the message of this parable.

Jesus' point is not to *compare* but to *contrast*. In other words, this story is not saying "God is like the judge" but "God is nothing like this judge." What is being contrasted in this story is the issue of inclination. The judge in the story is not inclined to help anyone or offer assistance in time of need. God, on the other hand, *is* inclined to participate in the lives of his children and help us in our need. His eye is on us, his ear is bent to hear us, his hand is outstretched, and his heart is tender toward his children. Jesus is saying: Look at this hard-hearted, uncaring judge … God is nothing like him.

Read Psalm 103:1 – 13

4. If God is the opposite of this judge in every way, what do we learn about:

- How God feels about us?

- God's inclination to hear us?

- God's willingness to answer prayer?

How does our theology of prayer change when we shift from comparing God to the judge to contrasting God to the judge?

5. In light of what you learn about God and prayer in this new reading of the parable, what do you think Jesus means when he says, "Always pray and do not give up"?

Contrast #2: We Are Not Like the Widow

In the parable we see that the widow is in a bad way. She doesn't have a chance. But, according to Jesus, she has a secret weapon: the power of pestering. Manipulating the judge with sheer irritation, she finally succeeds in having her petition granted. She gets what she is asking for not because the judge loves her, cares about her situation, or even because he is just—but only so she will leave him alone. If we are compared to the widow in this story, then Jesus is teaching that the only way to get prayer answered is to keep bugging God until he gets sick of us and gives in. Again, this is *not* the message of the parable.

The point, as before, is contrast, not comparison. We are nothing like the widow, who is penniless, powerless, desperate, alone, without connection or hope in the world. For those who follow Jesus, this will never be the case. We are loved by God, embraced as his children. We have free access to the throne room of the Father; his ear is inclined to hear our prayers ... the first time we ask.

Read John 1:12 – 13 and Romans 8:14 – 17

6. If we are nothing like the woman in the parable and she is meant to give us a picture of contrast, what do you learn about:

   • How God feels about us when we come to him in prayer?

- What kind of confidence we can bring when we approach God?

- Why God answers our prayers?

- How "hard" we have to pray to get God's attention?

7. If we really believe God is a perfect loving Father and we are his precious children, how might this impact the way we pray?

Why do you think God chooses to use the image of a loving Father to give us a picture of how he wants to relate to us?

When I Don't Get My Prayers Answered

When we make a specific request of God we don't always know how or when he will answer. But we are called to continue on in prayer even if the way he answers is a mystery to us. Consider the following simple but helpful tool to understand how God answers prayer:

Sometimes God says, "Slow." We tend to subconsciously put a note at the bottom of our prayer requests, "Please answer ASAP." We want everything to fall into place according to our time schedule. But God is not bound by our sense of timing or pressured by our urgency. He sees the big picture and knows there are times when an immediate answer would be exactly what we do not need. In these moments God says, "Slow." He teaches us patience and reminds us, "Those who wait on the Lord will renew their strength."

Sometimes God says, "No." We can be shortsighted and fail to see the long-term implications of some of our prayers. God sees everything and knows that we occasionally ask for things that are simply unhealthy. Like a child who keeps asking a parent for more candy, we don't always know what is best for us. As the years pass, a mature follower of Christ will look back on some prayers that received a, "No" from God and say, "Thank you, God, for being wise and loving enough to tell me that."

Sometimes God says, "Go." When we pray and the timing is right and the prayer is in tune with the heart of God, we get a green light. God says, "Go." We don't have to pound down his door or say the same thing over and over again. God hears, loves, cares, and is ready to answer our prayers. We all love it when God says, "Go." But his "Slow" or "No" answers are just as much a sign that he is at work on our behalf.

Read James 4:1 – 3 and Isaiah 40:31

> Yet those who wait for the LORD
> > Will gain new strength;
> They will mount up with wings like eagles,
> > They will run and not get tired,
> > They will walk and not become weary.
> > (Isaiah 40:31, NASB)

8. What are some of the challenges we face when God says, "Slow," and we have to walk through a time of waiting?

How does God use times of waiting to strengthen and grow us as his followers?

9. In his love, there are times God says, "No." What are some of the reasons God might answer one of our prayers with a loving but firm "No"?

Tell about a time God said "No" to one of your prayers and later, when you looked back, you were so thankful that he did.

10. Many followers of Christ have been wrongly taught that God is compelled to always say "Yes" to our requests. Imagine a parent who always told their toddler "Yes" no matter what the request. What would happen to this child?

God is a loving Father. How is his commitment to wisely tell us "Slow," "No," and "Go" more grace-filled than just answering "Yes" to every prayer?

11. Invite your small group to pray for you in *one* of the following ways:
    - Tell about a request for which God has asked you to wait and let them know how they can support you in prayer and with encouragement in this season of waiting.
    - Share that God has answered "No" to one of your recent requests and how you are struggling with his answer, how at this time it makes no sense to you. Invite them to pray for you to have wisdom and faith along the journey.
    - Describe a recent situation in which God has answered "Go" to one of your requests. Allow group members to rejoice with you in this answered prayer.

Celebrating and Being Celebrated

Use the reflections shared in response to question 11 to lead you in a time of group prayer, praising God for answered prayer and lifting up those requests for which we still await his reply.

Loving and Being Loved

God is a loving Father, our heavenly Abba. He cares more about us than we can begin to understand. Take time in the coming week to thank God for being your Father in heaven. Let him know that you trust his wisdom, even when he says "Slow" or "No."

Serving and Being Served

During this session your group members communicated about some of their prayers and needs at this time in their life. Consider serving them in *one* of the following ways:

- Set aside five minutes each morning for the next week to pray for the needs, concerns, and burdens of your group members.
- Write a note to one or more of your group members letting them know they are being uplifted in prayer.
- Give a group member a call this week and offer to pray for them over the phone.

Session One – Christian Etiquette
LUKE 14:7–14; 18:9–14

Question 1

We all know how this story ends — awkwardly! When the wedding party comes in, they get the table of honor. The guests who have wandered up to the head table will politely be asked to find another seat. The story in Jesus' day and our day will not be that different. As for breaking rules of etiquette, we have all done it. Sometimes people don't really care ... etiquette is not their deal. At other times, we cross the line and don't even know it. Some of these experiences are very embarrassing. Others are quite humorous.

Question 2

At the start of the passage we learn that Jesus told this parable because he observed how the guests had been picking out places of honor at the table. What was going on here? In those days, there was a certain protocol, much as there is whenever we attend a wedding reception or formal banquet today. The head table is for the honored guests. You only sit there with an invitation, or if you are so filled with presumption that you believe you always belong there.

There is also a cultural element we need to be aware of as we read this passage. In the ancient Middle East people did not have tall tables like we do, and they had no chairs. They actually reclined around the tables in a sitting position, laying on their side, or propped up on an elbow or a pillow. Obviously when they reclined their head was toward the table and their feet away from it. As you might imagine, this was a very intimate seating arrangement.

Jesus noticed something. When the dinner party guests, all Pharisees, came into the room, they had their eyes on the head table, knowing that their host had also invited Jesus to attend.

71

Wouldn't it be nice to be seen at the head table with Jesus, they must have thought, and so they stood around the head table hoping that they could find a place there. Jesus used this mealtime moment as a chance to teach about etiquette, but really he was teaching about the human heart.

One of the rules Jesus addressed was the breech of etiquette that comes when a person takes a seat of honor but is not a guest of honor. The second is when we invite people to our parties because of what we can get from them and gain from their presence. In both cases, there are deep spiritual lessons to be learned.

Questions 3–5

Jesus was bothered by social presumption because he knew that social presumptuousness unmasked a deeper issue of spiritual presumption. There is a direct correlation between a person who is haughty in social settings and the true condition of their spiritual life. A person who is truly broken and humble before God spiritually will evidence this by grace and compassion in their social behavior. Show me a person who is arrogant in public, and I will show you a person who has probably never truly learned humility before the Lord.

I don't think Jesus was all that bothered, truthfully, about dinner party etiquette. I think it was merely a springboard to focus on something that is absolutely distasteful in God's eyes: the disease of "spiritual presumptuousness." A spiritually presumptuous person is one who says, "I know I am going to heaven. How could God refuse a spiritual person like me?" It can even be a Christian who says, "I am such a model Christian. My life is in impeccable order. I am doing all the right things. I have all the right attitudes. I wonder why God isn't blessing me more."

Jesus is going after this sin because he wants to teach his followers a new way of living. It is the road of humility, thinking of others before ourselves. When presumption begins to die and true humility comes alive in our hearts and lives, everything changes.

Questions 6–8

Philippians 2, a passage about the willing humiliation of Jesus, ties in closely to the lesson Jesus is teaching here in Luke. Here were people scrambling for positions of preeminence yet the apostle Paul says, "[Jesus] did not consider equality with God something to be grasped, but [emptied himself], taking the very nature of a servant, being made in human likeness" (Philippians 2:6–7). Jesus served with such commitment and humility that he went all the way to the cross for us. In light of the example of Jesus, how could we live with such willful pride?

In Luke, Jesus is teaching that in order for us to understand Christian etiquette, we have to learn how to select the right seat at a dinner party—the cheap seat. The reason why we do this? People who have the heart of Jesus know that if they actually got what they deserved from God, it would be a whole lot less than the cheap seats at a banquet.

Questions 9–11

Jesus has another lesson in Christian etiquette: teaching us how to put together a guest list. He says, "Don't invite your friends, your brothers, your relatives, and your rich neighbors; they will just invite you back in return. Repayment will come." Instead Jesus explains that we find true blessing when we invite those who are outcasts and on the margins of society. These are the people who never get invited to parties.

The point is not that we should never have good friends, neighbors, or folks in a reciprocal relationship over for lunch. What Jesus is getting at is that the heart of God is broken for the marginalized, and our hearts should break too. When we have a heavenly perspective, we will realize that we are the broken and the outcast. Were it not for God's grace, we would never have been invited to his banquet table. So, when we know his love for us, we want to take action and extend this same care and grace to others.

This should propel the church, small groups, and each follower of Jesus to reach out to those who are often forgotten. This should cause us to connect with people in the marketplace or our neighborhood who have nothing to offer us, but God wants to offer them himself through us. A deep-rooted reality of God's love for us as outcasts should move our churches to serve the world. We should identify the most forgotten people and bring them the love, grace, and healing that are found in Jesus alone.

Session Two — Back to Basics
LUKE 14:25–33

Question 1

In Luke 14:25–33 Jesus takes us back to basics with words that are stark, sharp, and powerful. If you try to imagine how the people in the crowds that day felt when Jesus spoke these words, you might come up with terms like *shocked, confused, offended,* and *challenged*. Jesus knew the cross was on the horizon and he wanted the people to know that following him was not going to be an easy journey. It meant unparalleled devotion and radical sacrifice. Jesus was offering an off-ramp for those who were not ready for such a commitment.

Questions 2–3

In verse 25 we discover what prompts this discourse from Jesus. Large crowds were following Jesus. Most leaders want big crowds. In many cases, they don't even care about the motives and hearts of the crowd, as long as they show up, cheer, and make the leader feel good. But Jesus was concerned that people knew what it really meant to follow him. Half-hearted devotion was not going to sustain them in the coming days.

Jesus saw this as an ideal time to get back to the basics and remind people of three things:

- If you are going to follow me, no other human devotion can rival your love for me. Compared to your passion for me, all other loves should look like nothing, like you "hate" them. Wow, that would wake up the crowds.
- If you will be my disciple, you need to take the personal responsibility to carry the cross every day. You must be ready to follow and serve at a level that reflects a radical willingness to sacrifice at all times. Again, the crowds would have been taken aback.
- All those who would call themselves a Christian must take everything they own and place it on the altar. Hold nothing back. Make all your resources available for whatever needs God might point out.

You can almost hear Jesus say at the end of his teaching, "Okay, who still wants to hang out and follow me?" We have to wonder if the crowd thinned out a bit afterward.

Questions 4–6

Jesus was saying to his followers, "No other relationship should rival your love for me. You must value me more than your spouse, your children, your parents, and even your own life." That should have weeded out casual spectators. Jesus was not playing games. These were tough words. He was clear that love for God must take first place in our hearts and there should not be anyone in a close second place.

These words of the Savior are not just metaphors about loving God a lot. For some people they become very real. Muslims in many countries risk total abandonment by family and friends if they choose to follow Jesus. Even people who grow up in nonbelieving homes can count quite a cost when they say yes to Jesus and their life challenges the family norms. No matter what the cost, it is always right to follow God first.

Even Jesus had a chance to practice what he preached from this passage. At one point in his ministry Jesus made a statement that could be misunderstood as being dishonoring to his parents (Luke 8:19–21). Jesus was clear that his allegiance to his heavenly Father was greater than his commitment to earthly family.

Questions 7–8

It is a privilege to carry the cross of Jesus Christ—one of the most exciting and most fulfilling endeavors in life. Thankfully we are never called to carry it alone; God will be with us. Every time we bear the cross of Jesus we are empowered by the Holy Spirit. God will never assign a cross to us that the Spirit is incapable of enabling us to carry. If he says, "I want you to be a children's ministry leader or a small group leader," the Holy Spirit will enable you to be effective and to carry that cross with joy and effectiveness. The result will be the advancement of the kingdom of God, which thrills the heart of every true Christ follower. Also, we are told that there will be an eternal reward in heaven.

Questions 9–11

Both Jesus and the apostle Paul talk about the problem with loving money and material things. There is almost an emotional element to how we view money. Look at it this way. Imagine a guy who falls madly in love with a woman. He would do anything for her … swim oceans, climb mountains, all of that. He is obsessed with this angel in human form. She means everything to him. Then, six months after they begin dating, they break up. He "falls in love" with someone else and becomes totally wrapped up with her. Now he is swimming oceans and climbing mountains for his new love. How does this work? How can an old love just fade into history? How can a man who was "so in love" now say, "I can't even remember why I was so attracted to her" when he thinks of someone he was devoted to just a matter of months before? This is how God wants us to view the love of money and possessions. Let it go, forget it … and move on to a new love for the things of God.

Session Three – Lessons from Lazarus
LUKE 16:19–31

Question 1

Certain events raise deep issues that we tend to avoid in the rhythm of daily life. Funerals are one of those occasions when we are faced with the frailty of life and our own mortality, one of the times when we ask questions such as, "Is this life all there is?" and "What comes after it?" Jesus tells a story of two men who died and experienced radically different eternal states. Though many Christians today avoid talk of hell, Jesus does not. In this session we will learn from Lazarus and the rich man.

Questions 2–3

It is important that we understand the context in which Jesus told this story. Earlier in Luke 16, Jesus told the parable of the unjust steward, challenging the religious people of his day to realize that we can tell a lot about a person's heart by looking at their pocketbook or checkbook. How a person handles money unmasks things about values, ambitions, and priorities.

Jesus is not trying to communicate simplistic notions like: rich people go to hell and poor people go to heaven. He is not saying that all rich people are selfish and hard-hearted toward the plight of the poor. Jesus is teaching some profound truths about our hearts, eternity, and the reality of heaven and hell. Indeed, he is "meddling" in areas most wise people avoid, digging into topics most people would call "private." But with Jesus nothing is private; our whole lives are laid open before him.

Questions 4–6

One of the best ways to gain a healthy perspective on material goods (or anything we feel we possess) is to remember that all we have is a gift from God. Every spiritual gift, every ability, every possession, every opportunity, every good and perfect gift comes from God. We have nothing that has not been given by the grace of God.

When we understand that all we have is a gift, our attitude begins to change. We no longer feel that we deserve to live in splendor every day and experience excess at all times. We stop holding things in tight fists and we open our hands and say, "Lord, if you want to entrust me with affluence, I will humbly receive it, but I will keep my hands open to share it with others. And, if I only have a little in the eyes of this world, I will also hold that loosely and be ready to share with those in need." When times of plenty come, we are thankful. When lean times come, we agree with the apostle Paul when he commits to contentment with whatever he has.

If God chooses to give us a surplus of material goods we need to be on our guard. Jesus gave plenty of warnings about how wealth can corrupt our hearts and motives and become a rival love in our life. If we are not careful, affluence can breed insensitivity. This happens when we use our wealth as a buffer from the needs of the world. Those who have great financial resources can structure their life in a way that keeps them from having to deal with the plight of the poor and the heartache of the marginalized. Also, when a person is captured by a love for money and what it can buy, this sense of entitlement can allow them to justify that they deserve what they have, and the poor deserve what they are facing. The more money we have, the more we need to pay attention to these two temptations: excess and insensitivity.

Questions 7–8

In 1 Corinthians 15 the apostle Paul writes, in great detail, that the resurrection and hope of eternity with God are a source of strength and fortitude in the tough times of life. He says if there is no resurrection, no heaven, and no hope for the future, he would "eat, drink and be merry" (v. 32) because this world would be all there is. But Paul is clear that there is so much more. The resurrection of Jesus is real; Christians live with the promise of resurrection and the hope of heaven.

We live in a society that has been duped into thinking they are not going to die and give an account for their life. Many people do all they can to drink deep of this life because they think this is the whole deal. However, the Bible says true believers live with a constant awareness that they are going to die, and when they die, they are going to give an account of their lives. Because of the hope that Christ followers have in Jesus, they do not have to fear death.

As we look at Jesus' story of the rich man and Lazarus, we see three things: God's judgment is real and final; there is a chasm between heaven and hell that cannot be crossed; there are no second chances after death. Some arrogant people think they are going to cut a deal with God at the judgment. Not so, according to the Bible. We have one life to accept (and share) God's love and the hope and salvation that come in Jesus. We won't get a do-over some day in eternity.

Though no Christian takes delight in the reality of hell, we have to accept what the Bible teaches. It will be separation from God. It will involve torment. It is an eternal condition.

Questions 9–11

The rich man wants extraordinary measures implemented so that his five brothers will not end up in hell with him. But God's Word is clear: people have what they need to believe. There is an irony in the text when Abraham says, "If they do not listen to Moses and the Prophets, they will not be convinced even if someone rises from the dead" (Luke 16:31). In the context of the passage, Abraham is talking about the fact that the rich man's brothers won't change their lives and beliefs even if the rich man rises and goes to them. But Jesus is also alluding to his own eventual resurrection. And, just as he said, many still refuse to believe.

We have all we need to win family members, fellow workers, and neighbors to Jesus. What we have is the gospel. Not everyone will get it and accept it, but the message of God's love revealed in Jesus and infused with the power of the Holy Spirit is what people need. Paul says this message can seem like foolishness to some people, but we must bring it anyway, even if it means we look foolish in the eyes of the world.

Session Four – How to Receive a Miracle
LUKE 17:11–19

Question 1

One key in this session is to remember that miracles come in all shapes and sizes. As people tell their stories, be sure to celebrate the big and surprising miracles of God and also the daily ways that God can heal, restore, and lead us.

Question 2

If it were not for the healing power of Jesus, nothing the ten men could have done would have cleansed their skin. As they went, the miraculous power of God came upon them and their bodies were restored. Miracles are always due to the work and power of God.

At the same time, God invites us into the process. We have to identify our need and cry out to God. The Gospels portray this theme consistently. For some reason, God often waits until we ask for his power and help in our lives. Also, he will often give specific direction and instructions to those who want a miracle. Throughout the Old and New Testaments people were called to take a step of some sort. It is important to understand that we are partners with God in this process, but he is always the Senior Partner. Miracles are God's doing, but we can enter into what he wants to do through faith, crying out to him, and following his directions.

Questions 3–4

If we want to receive a miracle we need to bring our needs to Jesus and humbly ask for his help. Isn't it interesting that the ten lepers cried out for Jesus to have mercy on them? They asked for help. They knew Jesus could meet their deepest and most profound needs.

It would be nice to say that everyone will come to God and humbly ask for help, but this is not the case. For some reason, many people simply refuse to ask.

There are people who have serious needs, who know that Christ is available to help, who know that he is still on the throne, still has power, still cares ... but they refuse to cry out to him. Instead, they exhaust every human option they can think of. Sometimes after they have done all they can to fix their own life (in many cases quite unsuccessfully), they still refuse to humbly cry out for help from heaven. There are many reasons for this, among them: false humility (pride), a theology that denies God's power to heal or his interest in helping us, or a painful past that causes fear or hopelessness. Whatever the motivating factors, far too many people refuse to ask for God's help and thus miss out on the miracles he wants to do in their lives.

Questions 5–6

When the ten lepers cried out for help, it came in the form of specific directions from Jesus: go show themselves to the priests. When we cry out to God, he typically gives us some kind of direction to get us moving forward, toward his will and miracle. The direction might come from a Scripture that seems to jump right off the page and speak to our heart as an imperative. It can be an inner witness from the Holy Spirit, the counsel of a wise person, or multiple confirmations from a group of friends. God can even use situations and circumstances to provide a direction we need to take. One key is allowing for times of quietness and humility before God that invite him to give us direction. Too often we are so busy and distracted that we don't make space for God to speak to us.

Questions 7–8

When we cry out for God's direction and he gives it, we need to be ready to follow. At times it may seem unusual and illogical, but if we check it out with other believers and it squares with Scripture, we should follow the direction God gives. It is the pathway to the life of the supernatural, in which we are called to participate.

Sometimes we put potential miracles to death because we refuse to respond and move as the Spirit leads. We might have been quiet enough to receive God's direction, but when it comes we decline to follow because it doesn't square with our logic. If a leading from God seems financially, relationally, or vocationally risky, we bail out. Sadly, some of us have missed great adventures because we heard God's direction, but did not act on what we knew he was calling us to do.

God would like to have more of an entrance into our daily activities if we would only allow him access. If we lived with a ready and willing spirit, we could experience greater adventure, fruitfulness, and faithfulness. As we follow the story of the lepers, we discover that their miracle came *as they went*. Had they cried out, heard the instructions, but failed to begin the long walk to the priests, they would have never experienced healing.

Questions 9–11

Sometimes when God brings about a miracle, we miss it. Instead of giving him the praise and celebrating his great power and faithfulness, we just go on about our business. Some people look at a great work of God, a miraculous in-breaking of the Holy Spirit's power, and say, "What a coincidence," or, "This must be my lucky day." Worse yet, some people respond to God's miracles by saying, "It's about time. I really deserved something good happening in my life." In the story of the lepers, the majority report was a casual disregard for the One who had given them the miracle. But there was the one who came back to thank Jesus. What a glorious example! He said to himself, "I have a decision to make. Do I turn back and give God glory, or do I take my miracle and run?" He turned back. Not only did he come back, but he glorified God with a loud voice. He let everybody know.

Session Five — Becoming a Servant
LUKE 17:7–10; 12:35–40

Question 1

One of the greatest gifts God offers us is people who are filled with the Holy Spirit and who walk in a way that reflects Jesus himself. These are people we should celebrate. They are a blessing from heaven, tools in the hand of God to shape and form us into the people he wants us to be. When we are around people who are joyful servants, we experience the presence of Jesus.

Questions 2–3

To the casual observer all service can look the same. From the outside, serving is serving. But God's call for us to serve goes beyond an invitation to do an occasional good deed so that we can check "serving" off our list for the day. God is always concerned about our heart and motives. What he wants is for followers of Christ to actually be followers of Christ.

Jesus did not serve out of religious duty. He did not see his ministry in this world as a "to do" list with boxes to check off. Jesus came and served because he was compelled by love for us. He cared. When we fix our eyes on Jesus we discover that he was a servant at heart. As we understand this, we begin a journey from doing acts of service *because we are supposed to* to living as servants *because we love people the way Jesus did.*

Questions 4–6

Have you ever spent time analyzing why people do nice things for other people? Wonderful humanitarian gestures in this world are undertaken by believers and nonbelievers alike. Organizations such as United Way, the Peace Corps, Big Brothers and Sisters, and many others create excellent opportunities for serving. People give money for AIDS relief and research, cancer research, multiple sclerosis research, and so on. Local churches get involved in mission work, food programs, mentoring, tutoring, orphanages, hospitals, and much more. People all over the world are making a commitment to serve.

We should celebrate this. If people are extending compassion and care, this is a blessing. But it is also important that we take time to investigate our own motives for serving. We don't have to answer for others, but we are responsible for the condition of our own heart and life. The truth is, unhealthy motives for serving can subtly creep in if we're not careful.

Some people think that the only way they have a shot at gaining God's favor and covering over some sins of their past is by doing good things for others. Though the Bible is clear that no one will get into heaven through good works, this does not stop people from trying. Salvation is not through good works but the gift of grace found in Jesus.

Some people serve to get the applause of others. The praise of people becomes their fix—it is like a drug. The harder they work and the more they serve, the louder the applause. It becomes a vicious cycle. Jesus warns us not to practice our righteousness to impress people. He says that if others' praise is our hoped-for reward, it will be all we get. This motivation also leads to burnout. We can only serve people for so long before motivation fades. We end up saying, "He is not worth it. She is not worth it." When this happens, we will bail out on ministry.

Those who serve to satisfy some personal inner need will also lose motivation. Any effort to please self, discover self, or find self in service will become an empty pursuit. It is only in finding Jesus in service that it can become a joy-filled lifestyle.

People who serve out of guilt are always trying to figure out the minimum amount of service required to relieve their guilt. Their only goal is to alleviate their own pain, not to commit themselves unreservedly to another person or project or ministry. They are short-termers. As soon as their guilt is gone, they see no need for further service.

Questions 7–9

Rendering service and being a servant are worlds apart. Those who render service do a very good thing. There is nothing wrong with it. As a matter of fact, most people would improve their life if they were to render some kind of service each week. They would be more fulfilled and the world would be a better place. But God is calling his followers to something even more profound. He wants us to *become* servants. This means thinking in a new way. Serving becomes who we are, not just something we do on occasion. When we become servants, we become like Jesus.

Questions 10–11

God wants joy, one of the fruits of the Spirit, to mark the lives of his children. When serving brings us joy and we enter in with enthusiasm, we know that we are heading in the right direction. As serving becomes a natural expression of who we are, we are always ready to serve. We don't have to do an attitude check and then get ourselves all psyched up. As the servant heart of Jesus beats in our chest, we are always dressed for service because we never take off our skin … we *are* servants.

Session Six – Keep Praying
LUKE 18:1-8

Question 1

We all have seasons when praying feels more difficult, times when we're discouraged and making time to pray takes great effort. (We also experience times when we are so impassioned and excited about prayer that it just flows naturally.) It is helpful to be honest about this fact. For some people prayer becomes difficult because they have become too busy. For others it is a matter of sin and disobedience that makes prayer tough. In some cases it is fear, bad theology, or a series of prayers that seem to go unanswered. Whatever it is that keeps us from praying, when we identify it we begin a process of getting back on track with our prayer life.

Questions 2-3

Through the years many people have read this story as an allegory. It can feel like one. But if we force an allegorical interpretation we will end up with very poor theology. It is a parable and we need to be careful not to push every detail to have a one-to-one relationship to God and us as people who pray. To understand the right reading of this parable it is actually helpful to identify the wrong lessons.

In question 2 group members get a chance to do something that might feel strange: developing a wrong theology and interpretation of the passage. Some group members might feel uncomfortable with the implications of this method of interpretation, but when you shift to the correct meaning of the passage, it will all make sense.

Here are the shocking (and wrong) conclusions your group will arrive at by seeing God as the judge and us as the widow.

We have needs that aren't being met. We are getting no answer from heaven because God does not care about us. God invites us to pester him because it's the only way to get his attention and squeeze an answer out of him. If we pester and pester and pester, we are going to wear him down and at some point in time, he is going to say, "I can't stand it anymore. This person is wearing me out. I am sick of their whining. I'll give them what they want so they will go away and leave me alone." The moral of this story is pester, pester, pester and you will eventually wrench assistance out of a tight-fisted God. Of course, none of this is correct teaching about prayer.

Questions 4–5

The judge in this story is absolutely heartless and pagan. He does not fear God or people; he is insensitive and totally self-centered. Now, with that picture of a human judge in your mind, go as far as you can to the other side of the continuum and you start to get a picture of God. God cares, loves, listens, and is ready to help. The whole point of Jesus' parable is that God is the polar opposite of the judge. Whereas some parables are meant to create a comparison, this one is all about contrast. God is not like the judge; in fact, he is radically unlike him.

Psalm 103 captures the essence of God's nature; it is a beautiful picture of a God who is compassionate, sensitive, and sympathetic. He can empathize at the drop of a hat. He is gracious beyond our wildest imagination. He looks for excuses to show mercy. He is slow to anger. This does not mean he never becomes angry, but that his basic disposition is to be patient and long-suffering. Certainly unlike the judge in Luke 18.

There are two basics truths about prayer that every Christian should embrace. If we do, they will become like anchors to steady our soul in the tough times of life. The first truth is this: *the nature and the inclination of God's heart is to answer the prayers of his children.* We don't have to pressure, pester, or coerce God. He is already listening for our prayers and hears even the quietest whisper. He want to bless us, touch us, show us his power, and surprise us with his presence and grace. The second truth is closely related to the first: *we are loved children.* We are God's daughters and sons, not disconnected strangers. Through faith in Jesus we have been purchased, adopted into God's family, and loved more deeply than we could possibly dream.

Questions 6–7

Jesus paints the widow as a picture of total despair and hopelessness. In those days a widow was already marginalized, for in that culture a husband was vital for the welfare of a wife. The absence of her husband meant she was in big trouble. She probably had no income, no form of protection, very little status or power, no connections. (That is why in the New Testament the church is always encouraged to care for widows.) And on top of all this, this widow in this parable had an adversary who was out to get her. She was in a bad way.

Again, Jesus is creating a dramatic contrast (not a comparison). In essence he is saying, "You are nothing like this widow. You belong; you are loved; you have resources; you have an advocate; God is listening to you." The point is that we don't have to beg, manipulate, or pressure God. He is already listening. We are loved children. God is inclined to hear our needs and answer because he loves us.

Questions 8–11

The book of James warns us that sometimes our prayers go unanswered because we ask with wrong motives. We want the easy way out. We want the magic wand. But if our request is wrong, God will say, "No." Or he will say, "Grow." I firmly believe God withholds certain answers to prayers because he says, "You couldn't handle it. You need to trust me for a while. You need to walk in the dark until you get comfortable trusting me. I am not going to step in and bail you out. It's time to grow."

Because God loves us he is willing to say "Yes" to many of our prayers. He loves to answer in the affirmative. Because God loves us he sometimes says, "Slow." He knows we are not yet ready, so he waits and asks us to do the same. Sometimes the most loving thing God can do is call us to a process of waiting and maturing. There are even times when the loving heart of God demands a "No" answer to our request. If we are going to hurt ourselves, God will often lovingly say "No."

WILLOW
Willow Creek Association

Willow Creek Association
Vision, Training, Resources for Prevailing Churches

This resource was created to serve you and to help you build a local church that prevails. It is just one of many ministry tools that are part of the Willow Creek Resources® line, published by the Willow Creek Association together with Zondervan.

The Willow Creek Association (WCA) was created in 1992 to serve a rapidly growing number of churches from across the denominational spectrum that are committed to helping unchurched people become fully devoted followers of Christ. Membership in the WCA now numbers over 12,000 Member Churches worldwide from more than ninety denominations.

The Willow Creek Association links like-minded Christian leaders with each other and with strategic vision, training, and resources in order to help them build prevailing churches designed to reach their redemptive potential. Here are some of the ways the WCA does that.

- **The Leadership Summit**—a once a year, two-and-a-half-day conference to envision and equip Christians with leadership gifts and responsibilities. Presented live at Willow Creek as well as via satellite broadcast to over 130 locations across North America, this event is designed to increase the leadership effectiveness of pastors, ministry staff, volunteer church leaders, and Christians in the marketplace.

- **Ministry-Specific Conferences**—throughout each year the WCA hosts a variety of conferences and training events—both at Willow Creek's main campus and offsite, across the U.S., and around the world—targeting church leaders and volunteers in ministry-specific areas such as: small groups, preaching and teaching, the arts, children, students, volunteers, stewardship, etc.

- **Willow Creek Resources®**—provides churches with trusted and field-tested ministry resources in such areas as leadership, evangelism, spiritual formation, spiritual gifts, small groups, stewardship, student ministry, children's ministry, the use of the arts—drama, media, contemporary music—and more.

- **WCA Member Benefits**—includes substantial discounts to WCA training events, a 20 percent discount on all Willow Creek Resources®, *Defining Moments* monthly audio journal for leaders, quarterly *Willow* magazine, access to a Members-Only section on WillowNet, monthly communications, and more. Member Churches also receive special discounts and premier services through WCA's growing number of ministry partners—Select Service Providers—and save an average of $500 annually depending on the level of engagement.

For specific information about WCA conferences, resources, membership, and other ministry services contact:

Willow Creek Association
P.O. Box 3188
Barrington, IL 60011-3188
Phone: 847-570-9812
Fax: 847-765-5046
www.willowcreek.com

Just Walk Across the Room Curriculum Kit

Simple Steps Pointing People to Faith

Bill Hybels with *Ashley Wiersma*

In *Just Walk Across the Room*, Bill Hybels brings personal evangelism into the twenty-first century with a natural and empowering approach modeled after Jesus himself. When Christ "walked" clear across the cosmos more than 2,000 years ago, he had no forced formulas and no memorized script; rather, he came armed only with an offer of redemption for people like us, many of whom were neck-deep in pain of their own making.

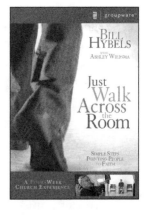

This dynamic four-week experience is designed to equip and inspire your entire church to participate in that same pattern of grace-giving by taking simple walks across rooms—leaving your circles of comfort and extending hands of care, compassion, and inclusiveness to people who might need a touch of God's love today.

Expanding on the principles set forth in Hybels' book of the same name, *Just Walk Across the Room* consists of three integrated components:

- Sermons, an implementation guide, and church promotional materials provided on CD-ROM to address the church as a whole
- Small group DVD and a participant's guide to enable people to work through the material in small, connected circles of community
- The book *Just Walk Across the Room* to allow participants to think through the concepts individually

Mixed Media Set: 978-0-310-27172-7

Pick up a copy at your favorite bookstore!

When the Game Is Over, It All Goes Back in the Box DVD

Six Sessions on Living Life in the Light of Eternity

John Ortberg with *Stephen* and *Amanda Sorenson*

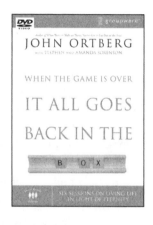

Using his humor and his genius for storytelling, John Ortberg helps you focus on the real rules of the game of life and how to set your priorities. *When the Game Is Over, It All Goes Back in the Box DVD* and participant's guide help explain how, left to our own devices, we tend to seek out worldly things, mistakenly thinking they will bring us fulfillment. But everything on Earth belongs to God. Everything we "own" is just on loan. And what pleases God is often 180 degrees from what we may think is important.

In the six sessions you will learn how to:

- Live passionately and boldly
- Learn how to be active players in the game that pleases God
- Find your true mission and offer your best
- Fill each square on the board with what matters most
- Seek the richness of being instead of the richness of having

You can't beat the house, notes Ortberg. We're playing our game of life on a giant board called a calendar. Time will always run out, so it's a good thing to live a life that delights your Creator. When everything goes back in the box, you'll have made what is temporary a servant to what is eternal, and you'll leave this life knowing you've achieved the only victory that matters.

This DVD includes a 32-page leader's guide and is designed to be used with the *When the Game Is Over, It All Goes Back in the Box* participant's guide, which is available separately.

DVD-ROM: 978-0-310-28247-1
Participant's Guide: 978-0-310-28246-4

Pick up a copy at your favorite bookstore!

The Case for Christ DVD

A Six-Session Investigation of the Evidence for Jesus

Lee Strobel and *Garry Poole*

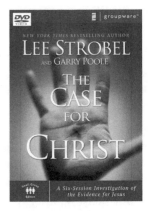

Is there credible evidence that Jesus of Nazareth really is the Son of God?

Retracing his own spiritual journey from atheism to faith, Lee Strobel, former legal editor of the *Chicago Tribune*, cross-examines several experts with doctorates from schools like Cambridge, Princeton, and Brandeis who are recognized authorities in their own fields.

Strobel challenges them with questions like:

- How reliable is the New Testament?
- Does evidence for Jesus exist outside the Bible?
- Is there any reason to believe the resurrection was an actual event?

Strobel's tough, point-blank questions make this six-session video study a captivating, fast-paced experience. But it's not fiction. It's a riveting quest for the truth about history's most compelling figure.

The six sessions include:

1. The Investigation of a Lifetime
2. Eyewitness Evidence
3. Evidence Outside the Bible
4. Analyzing Jesus
5. Evidence for the Resurrection
6. Reaching the Verdict

6 sessions; 1 DVD with leader's guide, 80 minutes (approximate).
The Case for Christ participant's guide is available separately.

DVD-ROM: 978-0-310-28280-8
Participant's Guide: 978-0-310-28282-2

The Case for a Creator DVD

A Six-Session Investigation of the Scientific Evidence That Points toward God

Lee Strobel and *Garry Poole*

Former journalist and skeptic Lee Strobel has discovered something very interesting about science. Far from being the enemy of faith, science may now provide a solid foundation for believing in God.

Has science finally discovered God? Certainly new discoveries in such scientific disciplines as cosmology, cellular biology, astronomy, physics and DNA research are pointing to the incredible complexity of our universe, a complexity best explained by the existence of a Creator.

Written by Lee Strobel and Garry Poole, this six-session, 80-minute DVD curriculum comes with a companion participant's guide along with a leader's guide. The kit is based on Strobel's book and documentary *The Case for a Creator* and invites participants to encounter a diverse and impressive body of new scientific research that supports the belief in God. Weighty and complex evidence is delivered in a compelling conversational style.

The six sessions include:

1. Science and God
2. Doubts about Darwinism
3. The Evidence of Cosmology
4. The Fine-tuning of the Universe
5. The Evidence of Biochemistry
6. DNA and the Origin of Life

The Case for a Creator participant's guide is available separately.

DVD-ROM: 978-0-310-28283-9
Participant's Guide: 978-0-310-28285-3

The Case for Faith DVD

A Six-Session Investigation of the Toughest Objections to Christianity

Lee Strobel and *Garry Poole*

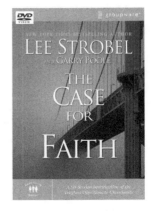

Doubt is familiar territory for Lee Strobel, the former atheist and award-winning author of books for skeptics and Christians. But he believes that faith and reason go hand in hand, and that Christianity is a defensible religion.

In this six-session video curriculum, Strobel uses his journalistic approach to explore the most common emotional obstacles to faith in Christ. These include the natural inclination to wrestle with faith and doubt, the troubling presence of evil and suffering in the world, and the exclusivity of the Christian gospel. They also include this compelling question: Can I doubt and be a Christian?

Through compelling video of personal stories and experts addressing these topics, combined with reflection and interaction, Christians and spiritual seekers will learn how to overcome these obstacles, deepen their spiritual convictions, and find new confidence that Christianity is a reasonable faith.

The Case for Faith participant's guide is available separately.

DVD-ROM: 978-0-310-24116-4
Participant's Guide: 978-0-310-24114-0

Pick up a copy at your favorite bookstore!

ZONDERVAN®
.com

ReGroup™

Training Groups to Be Groups

Henry Cloud, Bill Donahue, and John Townsend

Whether you're a new or seasoned group leader, or whether your group is well-established or just getting started, the *ReGroup™* small group DVD and participant's guide will lead you and your group together to a remarkable new closeness and effectiveness. Designed to foster healthy group interaction and facilitate maximum growth, this innovative approach equips both group leaders and members with essential skills and values for creating and sustaining truly life-changing small groups. Created by three group life experts, the two DVDs in this kit include:

- Four sixty-minute sessions on the foundations of small groups that include teaching by the authors, creative segments, and activities and discussion time
- Thirteen five-minute coaching segments on topics such as active listening, personal sharing, giving and receiving feedback, prayer, calling out the best in others, and more

A participant's guide is sold separately.

DVD: 978-0-310-27783-5
Participant's Guide: 978-0-310-27785-9

Pick up a copy at your favorite bookstore!

Share Your Thoughts

With the Author: Your comments will be forwarded to the author when you send them to *zauthor@zondervan.com*.

With Zondervan: Submit your review of this book by writing to *zreview@zondervan.com*.

Free Online Resources at
www.zondervan.com/hello

 Zondervan AuthorTracker: Be notified whenever your favorite authors publish new books, go on tour, or post an update about what's happening in their lives.

 Daily Bible Verses and Devotions: Enrich your life with daily Bible verses or devotions that help you start every morning focused on God.

 Free Email Publications: Sign up for newsletters on fiction, Christian living, church ministry, parenting, and more.

 Zondervan Bible Search: Find and compare Bible passages in a variety of translations at www.zondervanbiblesearch.com.

 Other Benefits: Register yourself to receive online benefits like coupons and special offers, or to participate in research.